Cambridge **Discovery Education**™

▶ **INTERACTIVE READERS**

Series editor: Bob Hastings

SURVIVAL GUIDE
LOST IN THE MOUNTAINS

A2+

Kathryn O'Dell

CAMBRIDGE
UNIVERSITY PRESS

University Printing House, Cambridge CB2 8BS, United Kingdom

One Liberty Plaza, 20th Floor, New York, NY 10006, USA

477 Williamstown Road, Port Melbourne, VIC 3207, Australia

314–321, 3rd Floor, Plot 3, Splendor Forum, Jasola District Centre, New Delhi – 110025, India

79 Anson Road, #06–04/06, Singapore 079906

Cambridge University Press is part of the University of Cambridge.

It furthers the University's mission by disseminating knowledge in the pursuit of education, learning and research at the highest international levels of excellence.

www.cambridge.org
Information on this title: www.cambridge.org/9781107643284

© Cambridge University Press 2014

First published 2014

20 19 18 17 16 15 14 13 12 11 10 9 8 7

Printed in Dubai by Oriental Press

A catalogue record for this publication is available from the British Library

Library of Congress Cataloging in Publication Data

O'Dell, Kathryn.
 Survival guide : lost in the mountains / Kathryn O'Dell.
  pages cm. — (Cambridge discovery interactive readers)
 ISBN 978-1-107-64328-4 (pbk. : alk. paper)
 1. Wilderness survival—Juvenile literature. 2. Mountains—Juvenile literature.
 3. English language—Textbooks for foreign speakers. 4. Readers (Elementary) I. Title.

GV200.5.O44 2013
613.6'9—dc23

                                    2013024136

ISBN 978-1-107-64328-4

Additional resources for this publication at www.cambridge.org

Layout services, art direction, book design, and photo research: Q2ABillSMITH GROUP
Editorial services: Hyphen S.A.
Audio production: CityVox, New York
Video production: Q2ABillSMITH GROUP

Contents

Before You Read: Get Ready! 4

CHAPTER 1
Getting Lost 6

CHAPTER 2
Getting Water 8

CHAPTER 3
Finding Food 12

CHAPTER 4
Finding Shelter 16

CHAPTER 5
Dangerous Terrain and Bad Weather 20

CHAPTER 6
What Do You Think? 24

After You Read 26

Answer Key 28

Glossary

Before You Read:
Get Ready!

Climbing in high, snowy mountains can be dangerous. It is even more dangerous if you get lost. This book tells you how to stay alive.

Words to Know

Look at the pictures. Then complete the sentences with the correct words.

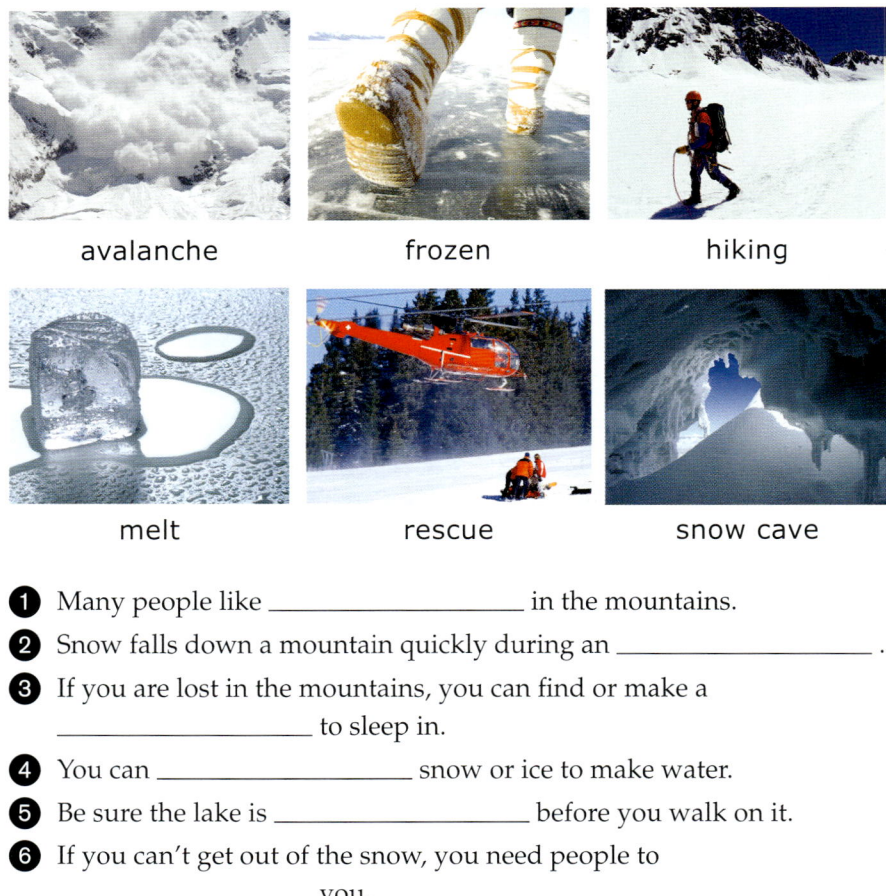

avalanche   frozen   hiking

melt   rescue   snow cave

1 Many people like _____ in the mountains.

2 Snow falls down a mountain quickly during an _____ .

3 If you are lost in the mountains, you can find or make a _____ to sleep in.

4 You can _____ snow or ice to make water.

5 Be sure the lake is _____ before you walk on it.

6 If you can't get out of the snow, you need people to _____ you.

Words to Know

Read the definitions. Then complete the diary with the correct form of the highlighted words.

energy: if someone has energy, he/she can do things without getting tired

pack: a bag that you carry on your back

shelter: a place that keeps you safe in bad weather or from danger

survive: keep living after almost dying or being in danger

survival: the state of living after almost dying or being in danger

Day 1

My friend Kayla and I are in the beautiful Swiss Alps. We are climbing to the top of Monte Rosa. It will take three days to go up. We are sleeping in our tents for ❶ _____ at night. We're carrying them in our ❷ _____.

Day 2

We climbed all day. It's a good thing we had food with us. We needed a lot of ❸ _____ to climb in the cold.

Day 3

We got to the top today. The view was amazing! When we started back down, it began to snow. We couldn't see, so we had to stay in one place. I thought we might not ❹ _____ the cold.

Day 4

It finally stopped snowing yesterday, but it was already dark. We started back down in the dark with lights on our hats. We finally found a safe place to camp. We slept for a few hours, and then we walked down the mountain this morning. Kayla says that I should write our ❺ _____ story and post it online!

CHAPTER 1

Getting Lost

IMAGINE BEING LOST IN THE MOUNTAINS.

The Alps is a mountain range that goes through France and seven other countries.

Imagine[1] you are in the French Alps. Maybe you are skiing or snowboarding down a mountain. Or perhaps you are a **hiker** on a walking tour, or even a skilled[2] mountain climber. It starts to snow. Suddenly, you don't know where you are. You can't find the people you are with. You are cold and lost in the Alps. What do you do?

Every year, people get lost in the Alps and other mountains around the world. Some people die, and others get hurt. Mountains can be very dangerous, especially when there's snow. Avalanches happen often. In one year, 80 tourists died in avalanches in the French Alps. About 35 people die in avalanches each year in the United States.

[1] **imagine:** make an idea in your head
[2] **skilled:** having what is needed to do something well

But avalanches aren't the only problem. Some people don't plan well. They don't have enough food or water. Others fall off the side of a mountain or into cold water. Sometimes people get caught in a bad snowstorm and die from the cold.

However, if you stay **calm** and have the right skills, you can survive. If you are lost, just remember the word STOP.

S = *Stop*. Stay calm.

T = *Think*. How did you get lost?
Can you get back?

O = *Observe*.[3] Where are you?
Does anything look familiar?[4]

P = *Plan*. What do you need to do to survive?

In 2011, Brock Besner and Craig D'Allessandro survived for three days during a terrible snowstorm in high mountains. Keep reading to learn how they did it and how you can survive if you are ever lost in the mountains.

---

[3] **observe:** watch something carefully
[4] **familiar:** describing something you know well or have seen before

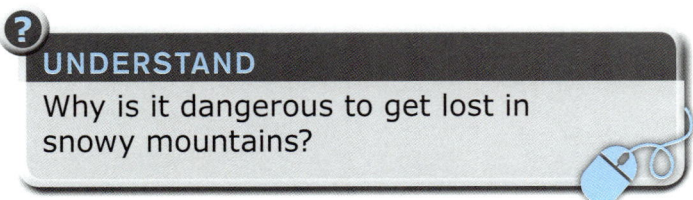

?

UNDERSTAND
Why is it dangerous to get lost in snowy mountains?

CHAPTER 2

Getting Water

HOW WILL YOU GET WATER IF YOU ARE LOST?

If you are planning to be in snowy mountains, you need to bring water or have ways to get it. You should drink more than one liter of water every day. If you are on a day **hike**, skiing, or snowboarding, you should bring a two-liter bottle of water with you. If you are planning a longer stay, you should still only bring two liters. More water will make your pack too heavy.

When you need water, you can get it from lakes and rivers or by melting snow. You should **boil** the water before you drink it, so don't forget to bring a lighter or matches to start a fire. You can also bring tablets that you put in water to make it safe, or you can bring a water filter.

You may be asking, "Why is water unsafe? Water in the mountains is cleaner than water in the city, right?" This isn't always true. For example, in the lower part of the Alps, there are many animals, and they can contaminate[5] the water.

You can start a fire with a lighter or matches.

Drinking unsafe water can give you stomach problems. It can make you sick for a day or two or even for a few weeks. Water can be clean, especially high in the mountains. But even if the **risk** is low, you don't want to be sick when you are hiking

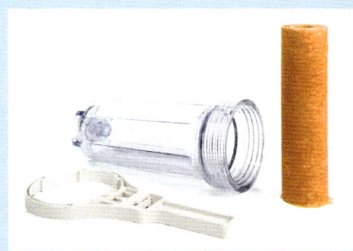

You can use a water filter to make water safe to drink.

or doing sports in the mountains. And you *really* don't want to get sick if you are lost in the mountains, so it is always best to purify[6] water before drinking it.

[5] **contaminate:** make something dangerous or dirty
[6] **purify:** make something clean

tinder

kindling

How do you purify water in the mountains? First, get some water from lakes or rivers, or use snow if there is no water nearby. Next, make a fire and heat the water until it boils. It sounds easy, doesn't it? But it's not so easy to make a fire in the mountains. Here's how to do it:

1　Find a place that is dry and out of the wind.

2　Put down some dry tree **branches**.

3　Put tinder (twigs,[7] dead leaves, dry grass) on the branches.

[7] **twig:** a small thin branch of a tree

4 Light the tinder with a lighter or matches, and then add kindling (small, dry branches).

5 When the kindling is burning well, add some more dry wood.

If you don't have matches or a lighter, you can start a fire with a dry branch and a flat piece of wood. Turn the branch around and around really fast on the wood until it gets hot and starts to smoke. Then hold your tinder close to the branch until it catches fire. It's not easy, but keep trying, and it will work in the end.

If you're lost in the mountains with no water and you can't make a fire, then you should use your body heat to melt snow. Put some snow in a water bottle and leave it under your jacket while you walk or sleep at night. The snow will melt, but the water won't be purified.

If, however, you have no other water to drink you should take the risk and drink it. If you don't drink enough water, your body becomes dehydrated, which is a serious problem and can even cause people to die.

[8] **flint:** a kind of rock used to start a fire

Video Quest

Making Spruce Tea

In this video, Bear Grylls uses a flint[8] to make a fire in the French Alps. How does he melt snow?

CHAPTER 3

Finding Food

WHAT FOOD CAN YOU EAT IN THE MOUNTAINS?

Beef jerky is a high-energy food.

When you plan to be in the mountains for a long time, you don't want to carry a heavy pack. You should bring food that is high in energy but low in **weight**. It's also a good idea to bring food that is easy to prepare and that won't spoil[9] if it gets frozen.

Even if you are on a day hike, you need to bring some food. When you climb a mountain, your body uses more energy, so you may need to eat twice as much as usual.

Good foods to take along when you're hiking

Dehydrated Foods	Instant[10] Foods	Other
beef jerky	potatoes	fish in a can
dried fruits	soup mix	crackers
dried fish	milk	cheese

[9] **spoil:** become bad to eat
[10] **instant:** something that can be made quickly by adding water

What can you do if you are lost in snow-covered mountains and you have no food left? Because it is so cold, not much grows high in the mountains. It can be very difficult to find food there. However, if you know what to look for, there are plants you can eat.

You can eat the roots of some trees, like pine trees. They give you a lot of energy. In spring, you can also eat the buds[11] from some trees. They won't give you much energy – about the same as eating a small piece of chocolate – but they may give you enough energy to keep looking for other food.

[11] **bud:** a flower or leaf of a tree before it opens

? EVALUATE
What other foods do you think would be good for a long hiking trip?

You can eat pine tree roots.

A mealworm

If you're really hungry, you can look for maggots[12] and insects. Some ants are good to eat. Others are **poisonous**, but you can eat their eggs. You can also eat mealworms. Look for them under rocks and fallen trees. Mealworms often taste like the food they last ate! You can cook mealworms over a fire, but for a quick meal, you can eat mealworms without cooking them.

If you have a net,[13] use it to catch fish in a river or lake. If you don't have a net, you can make a fishing line with things in your pack, like **string**. If the water isn't deep, you can even fish with your hands.

[12] **maggot:** an animal with a soft body that later becomes a fly
[13] **net:** something used for catching or holding things

You can eat animals if you can catch one. It's probably not as difficult as you think. If you have wire, you can make a snare. If not, you can make a deadfall trap. But remember small animals are best. It's not a good idea to try to catch large animals like bears!

 **How to make a wire snare**	 **How to make a deadfall trap**
Make a circle with wire. **Tie** one end to a tree. When an animal runs through it, the circle will get smaller and catch it.	Prop up[14] a large rock with tree branches. Put one of the branches where an animal could walk over it. When the animal walks over the branch, the rock will fall and kill it.

[14] **prop up:** lift and hold something by putting something under it

Video Quest

Eating in the Alps

Watch this video to learn how to eat in the French Alps. How does the man catch fish?

CHAPTER 4

Finding Shelter

WHERE WILL YOU SLEEP IF YOU ARE LOST FOR MORE THAN A DAY?

In some mountain areas there are special cabins[15] where hikers can sleep. But most hikers have to camp. And that means taking the right camping equipment[16] in your pack.

The first thing you should have is a tent. You also need a sleeping bag. Get a sleeping bag that is warm but light in weight.

What to think about when buying a good snow tent

- It needs to be good in strong winds.
- It should **weigh** less than 1.5 kilograms.
- It should have a dome shape.

[15] **cabin:** a small house made of wood
[16] **equipment:** things you need to do something

But what do you do if you get lost and do not have a tent? It is important to find a warm place to sleep. If you sleep outside in freezing weather, your body loses heat, and you can get hypothermia – when your body's temperature is less than it should be.

Snow falls off a dome-shaped tent.

Hypothermia can kill you. Normal body temperature is 37° C. Hypothermia starts when the body's temperature goes below 35° C. Even at just below 35° C, the body can have heart problems and the brain can stop working.

You must stay warm, so you need to make a shelter to sleep in. Make your shelter on the side of the mountain that has gotten sun during the day. Then find some long, thick branches to make a tree shelter. Put the branches against a tree or near a tree in the shape of a tent. Then cover the shelter with leaves or even snow. This will keep out the wind, rain, and snow.

If you have clothing or a blanket, put it on the ground. You lose a lot of body heat through the ground. If you have a hat, wear it. You also lose body heat through your head.

A tree shelter can keep you warm at night.

If there are no trees, try to find a snow cave. You can also make a snow cave by digging a hole in the snow.

A snow cave will keep you out of the cold and wind. Your cave should be about three times the size of your body. If it is too big, the heat that your body gives off in the night will be lost. If it is too small, it may fall down on top of you while you're sleeping.

A tree shelter or a snow cave can also protect you from animals, which might be out at night. If you have any food, be sure it is covered well and inside your shelter. This way animals like bears won't smell it.

Video Quest

Making a Snow Cave

Watch this video to see how Bear Grylls makes a snow cave in the Alps. How does he make it?

CHAPTER 5

Dangerous Terrain and Bad Weather

HOW CAN YOU STAY SAFE WHILE WALKING IN THE SNOW AND ICE?

When you walk on dangerous terrain,[17] it's easy to fall and get hurt. So it's important to wear good, comfortable boots. You should also wear wool socks to keep your feet warm and dry.

If you are climbing high mountains, bring crampons. These go on the bottom of your boots and make it easier to climb on ice. It's also a good idea to have trekking poles. These help you walk on snow and ice. Trekking poles also help you walk farther—they make you use your arms more, and your legs don't get so tired. If you don't have trekking poles, use a long branch instead.

Crampons go on your boots.

[17] **terrain:** the type of land. Terrain can be rocky or flat, etc.

Trekking poles

Other useful items for hikers

- sunblock
- clothing that dries quickly
- a hat
- sunglasses
- a knife
- a light
- a cup

It is difficult to walk in deep snow because your body sinks[18] in it. Snowshoes can help you walk on top of the snow. They are much bigger than boots and cover a larger area of snow, so you don't sink as easily.

If you don't have snowshoes with you, you can make them from tree branches and string. Make the outside of the snowshoe with the branches. Then tie the string from one side to the other, again and again, to make a place for your foot. Then tie the snowshoes to your boots.

[18] **sink:** go down through something

Another danger in the mountains is frozen rivers and lakes. They might not be completely frozen, and you could fall through the ice. If you have to walk on frozen water, walk close to the edge.[19] This way, if you fall in, you can get to the side and pull yourself out. Stay calm. If you aren't calm, you could drown.[20]

When you get out of the water, you must take your clothes off quickly. Wet, cold clothes are very dangerous, and you could get hypothermia. If you don't have other clothes to put on, start a fire and dry your clothes by the fire. Be sure to dry your socks and boots, too.

[19] **edge:** the part around something that is farthest from the center

[20] **drown:** die under water

Avalanches are very dangerous. Often they are started by skiers, snowboarders, and people on snowmobiles,[21] but hikers should also be careful not to start avalanches.

Avalanches often happen after a snowstorm, when the temperature goes up quickly, and when it is windy. During these times, stay away from open areas and walk near rocks or trees.

How to survive an avalanche

- Let go of anything you're carrying.
- If you can, move to the side to get out of the path of the avalanche.
- Stay on your feet if you can.
- If you can't stand up, try to "swim" in the snow, by moving your arms.
- Hold on to a tree if one is near you.

[21] **snowmobile:** a motorbike that travels on snow or ice

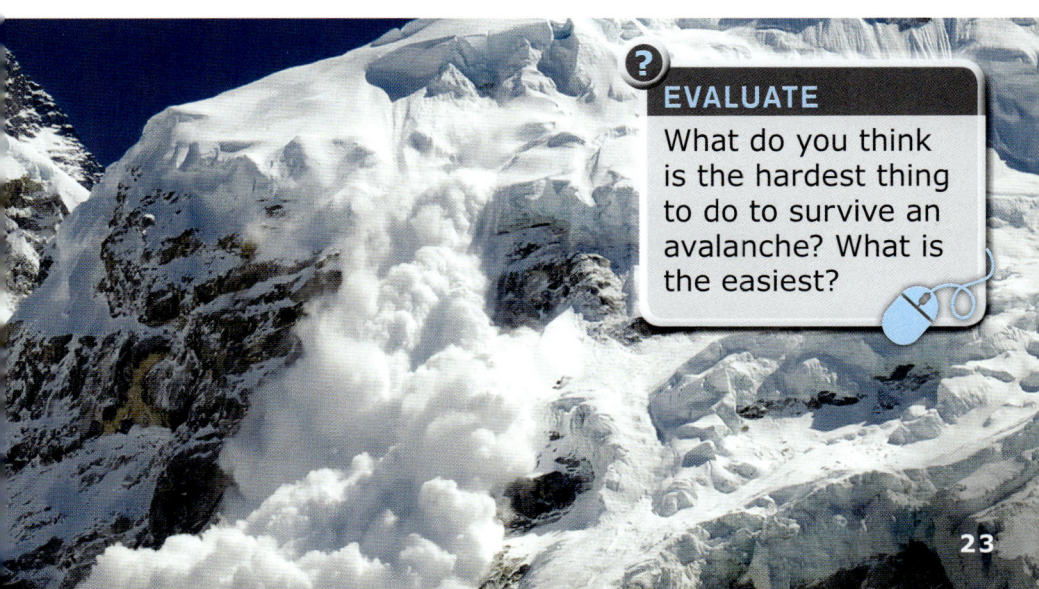

? EVALUATE

What do you think is the hardest thing to do to survive an avalanche? What is the easiest?

CHAPTER 6

What Do You Think?

COULD YOU SURVIVE IN THE MOUNTAINS?

Imagine you are lost in the mountains. You don't know where you are. There's no one to help you. You can't get back to safety. Could you survive long enough for rescue workers to find you?

The first thing to remember is this: always tell someone where you're going. Many people are saved because their friends and family tell rescue workers they are missing.

If you need to be rescued, tie a piece of clothing to a long branch. Put it in a clear area for others to see. Also, use your feet or tree branches to make a large X or the letters SOS in the snow. Rescue workers may see this from a helicopter.

What other ways can you think of to show rescue workers where you are? When is it better to try to find your own way back? When is it better to stay in one place and wait for help?

Remember Brock and Craig who were caught in a terrible snowstorm in 2011? How did they survive?

They knew they could not find their way to safety because of the snowstorm, so they walked to some trees and stayed there. They had a little food with them, so they ate some beef jerky. They also made a fire with tree branches to stay warm and to melt snow for water. They dug a snow cave, and they slept in it for two nights. On the third day, rescue workers found them. Brock and Craig were lost in the mountains. They were in danger, but they survived.

Why do you think Brock and Craig survived? Could you do what Brock and Craig did? Could you survive in the mountains?

After You Read

Read the sentences and choose Ⓐ, Ⓑ, or Ⓒ.

1 What is the first thing you should do if you get lost in the mountains?
- Ⓐ Plan what you need to do to survive.
- Ⓑ Stop and stay calm.
- Ⓒ Observe what is around you.

2 How can you make water safe to drink?
- Ⓐ Drink it directly from a river or lake.
- Ⓑ Boil it, filter it, or put tablets in it.
- Ⓒ You cannot make water safe to drink.

3 What is the best kind of food to take on a long hike?
- Ⓐ Food that is heavy and gives you energy.
- Ⓑ Food that is light and gives you energy.
- Ⓒ Fresh fruits and vegetables.

4 Where can you find food in the snowy mountains?
- Ⓐ In the snow or on ice.
- Ⓑ On top of a frozen lake.
- Ⓒ Near trees or under water.

5 What does Bear Grylls use the maggots for?
- Ⓐ He eats them and catches fish with them.
- Ⓑ He uses them to start a fire.
- Ⓒ He makes tea with them.

6 What is hypothermia?
- Ⓐ When your brain stops working.
- Ⓑ When you have heart problems.
- Ⓒ When your body loses heat.

7 What is a good shelter at night if you're lost in the mountains?
- Ⓐ A blanket and a hat.
- Ⓑ An opening between trees.
- Ⓒ A tree shelter or a snow cave.

Complete the Chart

Put the words in the correct place in the chart.

cabin	fish	insects	kindling	lighter
plants	snow cave	tinder	tree shelter	

Things to make a fire	Shelter	Food you can eat
_____	_____	_____
_____	_____	_____
_____	_____	_____

Complete the Text

Complete the story with the correct words from the box.

freezing	hike	melt	shelter	survived

   In 2011, Lauren Weinberg, a 23-year-old college student from Arizona, USA, was driving her car in the mountains when she got stuck in the snow. It was too far to ❶ _____ to safety, so she decided to stay in the car. It was her only ❷ _____ from the snow and ❸ _____ temperatures. It was about –17° C at night!

   The only food she had was two candy bars. She put snow in a water bottle to ❹ _____ it, so she had water to drink. Rescue workers finally found her. She ❺ _____ for 10 days alone in the car!

Short Answer

You are lost in the desert in hot weather. What do you do to survive? How are the problems the same as when you are lost in the snowy mountains? How are they different?

Answer Key

Words to Know, page 4

1 hiking **2** avalanche **3** snow cave **4** melt **5** frozen
6 rescue

Words to Know, page 5

1 shelter **2** packs **3** energy **4** survive **5** survival

Understand, page 7

There could be an avalanche. You could not have enough food or water. You could fall off the mountain or into cold water. You could get too cold.

Video Quest, page 11

He puts snow on a branch. He puts the branch into a snow bank near the fire. He puts a cup under the ball of snow.

Evaluate, page 13 *Answers will vary.*

Video Quest, page 15

He makes a fishing line with maggots on it. He puts the line through a hole in the ice.

Video Quest, page 19

He digs a hole in the snow with a piece of plastic.

Evaluate, page 23 *Answers will vary.*

Choose the Correct Answers, page 26

1 B **2** B **3** B **4** C **5** A **6** C **7** C

Complete the Chart, page 27

Fire: lighter, kindling, tinder; Shelter: cabin, snow cave, tree shelter; Food: insects, fish, plants

Complete the Text, page 27

1 hike **2** shelter **3** freezing **4** melt **5** survived

Short Answer, page 27 *Answers will vary.*